Maths Problems

and

Investigations

for 5–7 Year Olds

Greg Purcell

We hope you and your pupils enjoy the activities in this book. Brilliant Publications publishes many other books for teaching maths. To find out more details on any of our titles please log onto our website: www.brilliantpublications.co.uk.

Maths Problems and Investigations for 7–9 Year Olds
Maths Problems and Investigations for 9–11 Year Olds
Maths Problem Solving Year 1   Maths Problem Solving Year 4
Maths Problem Solving Year 2   Maths Problem Solving Year 5
Maths Problem Solving Year 3   Maths Problem Solving Year 6
Maths Builder Series: Fractions and Decimals; Multiplication; Addition; Subtraction; Division

Published by Brilliant Publications
Unit 10,
Sparrow Hall Farm,
Edlesborough,
Dunstable,
Bedfordshire,
LU6 2ES

Website: www.brilliantpublications.co.uk
E-mail: info@brilliantpublications.co.uk
Tel: 01525 222292
Fax: 01525 222720

The name 'Brilliant Publications'
and the logo are registered trade marks.

Written by Greg Purcell
Illustrated by Tim Higgins
Cover illustration by Brilliant Publications
Printed in the UK.

© 2012 Greg Purcell and Brilliant Publications
Printed ISBN: 978-0-85747-626-5
e-book ISBN: 978-0-85747-682-1
First published 2012
10 9 8 7 6 5 4 3 2 1

The right of Greg Purcell to be identified as the author of this work has been asserted by himself in accordance with the Copyright, Designs and Patents Act 1988.

Pages 5–44 are photocopiable. These pages have the phrase 'This page may be photocopied for use by the purchasing institution only' written at the bottom of each. They may be photocopied by the purchasing institution or individual teachers for classroom use only, without consent from the publisher and without declaration to the Publishers Licensing Society. The material in this book may not be reproduced in any other form or for any other purpose without the prior permission of the publisher.

Contents

Introduction		4
1	Number	5
2	Addition	6
3	Subtraction	7
4	Multiplication	8
5	Division	9
6	Fractions	10
7	Data	11
8	Length	12
9	Area	13
10	Volume and capacity	14
11	Mass	15
12	Time	16
13	Number	17
14	Addition	18
15	Subtraction	19
16	Multiplication	20
17	Division	21
18	Fractions	22
19	Data	23
20	Number operations	24
21	Patterns	25
22	Length	26
23	Area	27
24	Volume and capacity	28
25	Mass	29
26	Time	30
27	Number	31
28	Addition	32
29	Subtraction	33
30	Multiplication	34
31	Division	35
32	Fractions	36
33	Data	37
34	Patterns	38
35	Addition	39
36	Subtraction	40
37	Multiplication	41
38	Division	42
39	Fractions	43
40	Data	44
Answers		45–48

Introduction

Maths Problems and Investigations is a series of three books presented in stages across the primary grades. The purpose of each book is to engage the students in problem-solving activities whereby children:

- read the problem
- identify relevant information
- select appropriate strategies
- solve the problem
- check the reasonableness of their solutions

On most pages, problems are presented as Step 1, Step 2 and as an investigation.

Step 1
These problems are generally one-step problems requiring one mathematical operation with language that indicates the required operation.

Step 2
These problems involve more sophisticated language and may involve more than one operation in order to calculate the answer.

Investigations
The investigations are designed to represent real-life situations.
To successfully solve the investigations, children demonstrate:

- ability to think and work mathematically
- knowledge of a range of mental and written strategies
- overall competence in mathematics

Appropriate strategies
Children as young learners need to both be shown and experience a variety of mental strategies, as well as traditional written strategies. Such strategies include:

- *Estimation.* So that if the solution differs from the initial estimate, the answer might need to be checked or an alternative strategy employed.

- *Written.* Problems involving large numbers and those that require two or three steps in order to reach a solution are best solved using pencil and paper strategies. Answers can be checked and reworked if necessary.

- *Calculator.* Competent use of a calculator demonstrates mathematical competence and forms a legitimate problem-solving strategy.

1 Number

Step 1

My strategies

1	There are three bundles of 10 pencils. How many pencils are there?	
2	Find an odd number between 4 and 6.	
3	Find an even number between 16 and 20.	

Step 2

2 8 12 14

My strategies

1	In a pattern of 2s, what comes after 18?	
2	In a pattern of 2s, what comes before 40?	
3	In a pattern of 5s, what comes after 45?	

Investigation   What number am I?

Clues

I have two digits.
I am an even number.
I am less than 20.
I am greater than 13.
I am less than 16.

I have two digits.
I am an odd number.
I am greater than 23.
I am less than 27.

2 Addition

Step 1

My strategies

1	My first throw was a **5** and my second throw was a **4**. What is my total score?	
2	I had £3 and my dad gave me £2. How much have I got now?	
3	I had 6 points and then I got 4 more. How many points do I have now?	

Step 2

My strategies

1	How many stairs are there if I have already climbed 7 and I have 6 more to climb?	
2	How many balloons did we blow up altogether if William blew up 8 and Alex blew up 5?	
3	How many cups are on the shelf if there are 12 pink ones and 4 blue ones?	

Investigation   How to make 20

Find 3 pairs of numbers that make 20.

_____ + _____ = 20

_____ + _____ = 20

_____ + _____ = 20

6   Maths Problems and Investigations 5–7 Year Olds   ©Greg Purcell and Brilliant Publications
This page may be photocopied for use by the purchasing institution only.

3 Subtraction

Step 1

My strategies

1	I had £9 and spent £4. How much money have I got left?	
2	8 birds landed in the tree. The cat frightened 6 of them away. How many birds are left?	
3	I blew up 10 balloons but 6 burst. How many good ones do I have now?	

Step 2

My strategies

1	Mum bought 12 apples. How many are left if we ate 5 of them?	
2	I bought a packet of 15 party hats. How many are left over if we used 9 of them?	
3	I was given 13 pens but 3 didn't work. How many pens did work?	

Investigation   Robot bits

How many shapes would be left if I took away all the cubes?

How many shapes would be left if I took away all the rectangular prisms?

How many shapes would be left if I took away all the cylinders?

4 Multiplication

Step 1

My strategies

1	How many blocks are there? Lily has 2 rows of blocks with 4 blocks in each row.	
2	How many apples are in the shop window? There are 3 rows with 4 apples on each row.	
3	How many pencils does Luke have? He has 2 packets with 5 pencils in each packet.	

Step 2

My strategies

1	How many hairclips did I buy? I bought 2 packets with 3 hairclips in each packet.	
2	How many flowers does Lucy have? She has 2 bunches with 6 flowers in each bunch.	
3	How many books are on the shelves? There are 3 shelves with 5 books on each shelf.	

Investigation   Taxi ride

Each taxi can carry 5 people.

How many people can fit in 3 taxis?

How many people can fit in 4 taxis?

How many people can fit in 5 taxis?

5 Division

Step 1

My strategies

☐	How many pencils are in each group if I shared 8 pencils into 2 equal groups?	
☐	How many paintbrushes will each person get? I shared 10 paintbrushes equally between 2 people.	
☐	Grace and Ruby were given 6 stickers to share equally. How many will each person get?	

Step 2

My strategies

☐	9 trees were planted in 3 equal rows. How many will be in each row?	
☐	Ali and Rylan have £8 to share equally. How much will each person receive?	
☐	12 toys were put into 3 equal groups. How many toys will be in each group?	

Investigation   Balloons

Help the clown share 12 balloons.

12 balloons shared among 3 people.

12 balloons shared among 4 people.

12 balloons shared among 6 people.

©Greg Purcell and Brilliant Publications   Maths Problems and Investigations 5–7 Year Olds
This page may be photocopied for use by the purchasing institution only.

6 Fractions

Step 1

My strategies

1	Half of all the children were boys. How many boys were there if there were 8 children altogether?	
2	Half the children were girls. How many girls were there if there were 6 children altogether?	
3	Ava blew out one quarter of the 8 candles. How many candles did Ava blow out?	

Step 2

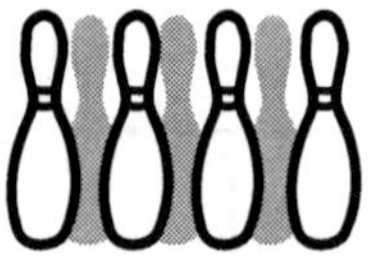

My strategies

1	In the bowling game half of the pins were knocked down. How many were still standing if there were ten pins altogether?	
2	12 birds landed in a tree. One quarter of them then flew away. How many were left?	
3	16 people came to my party. Half of them go to my school. How many people from my school came to my party?	

Investigation   Cup cakes

Mum made 16 cup cakes.

Draw a cherry on the top of ½ of the cakes.

How many cakes are in ½ of the group?

How many cakes are in ¼ of the group?

Is 9 more than half of the group?

10   Maths Problems and Investigations 5–7 Year Olds   ©Greg Purcell and Brilliant Publications
This page may be photocopied for use by the purchasing institution only.

7 Data

Animals at the zoo

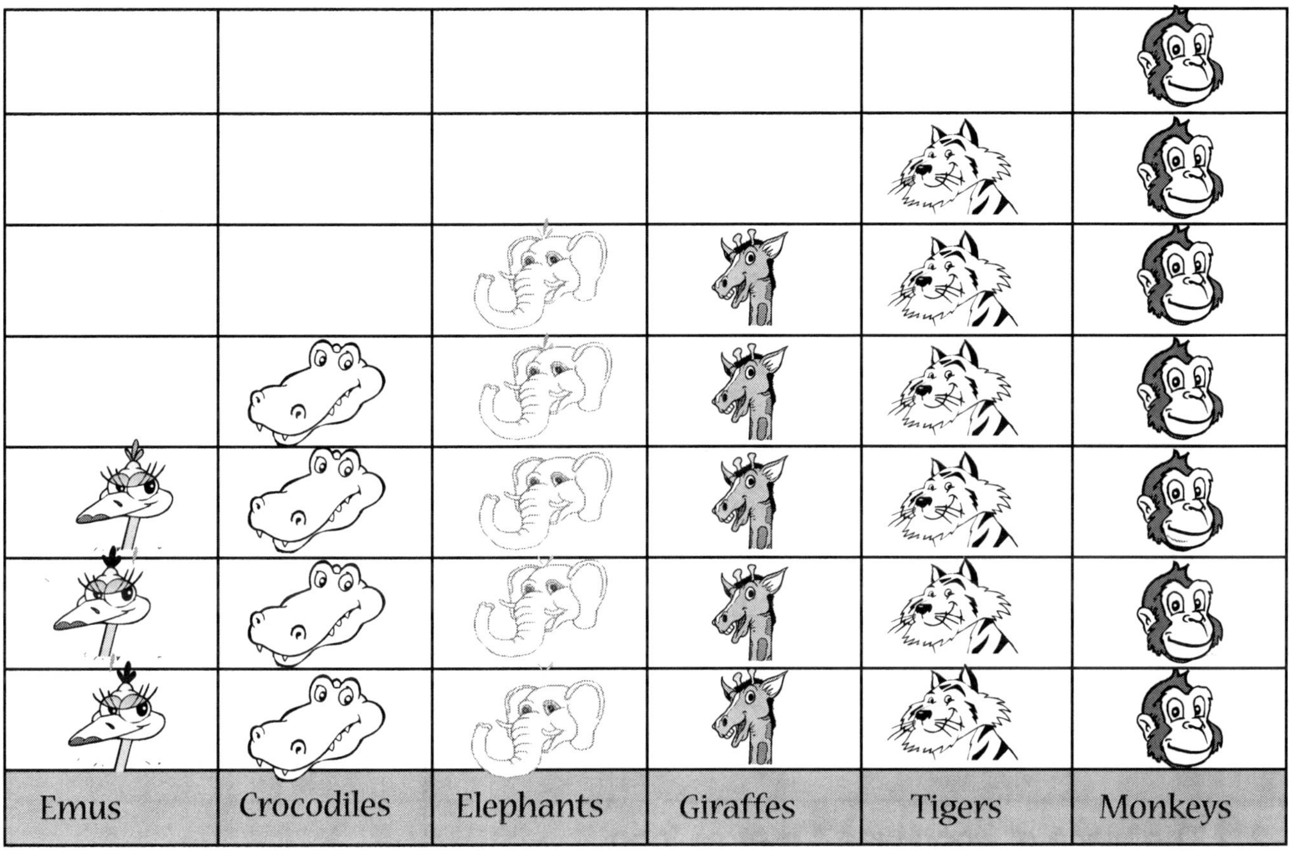

					🐵
				🐯	🐵
		🐘	🦒	🐯	🐵
	🐊	🐘	🦒	🐯	🐵
🦆	🐊	🐘	🦒	🐯	🐵
🦆	🐊	🐘	🦒	🐯	🐵
🦆	🐊	🐘	🦒	🐯	🐵
Emus	Crocodiles	Elephants	Giraffes	Tigers	Monkeys

Step 1

My strategies

1	How many animals are in the smallest group?	
2	How many animals are in the largest group?	
3	How many more monkeys are there than tigers?	

Step 2

My strategies

1	What is the difference in size between the largest group and the smallest group?	
2	How many more tigers are there than crocodiles?	
3	How many animals are there altogether?	

©Greg Purcell and Brilliant Publications   Maths Problems and Investigations 5–7 Year Olds
This page may be photocopied for use by the purchasing institution only.

8 Length

Step 1

My strategies

1	Our path is 6 metres long. If Dad adds another 3 metres, how long will it be?	
2	Jo's pencil is 8 centimetres long. If she broke off 2 centimetres, how long would it be?	
3	The giant's step is 3 metres long. How far would he travel if he took 3 steps?	

Step 2

My strategies

1	Each building block is 2 cm tall. How tall would a tower of 5 blocks be?	
2	The piece of wood was 4 metres long. How much is left if I chop half off?	
3	Eva lives 3 kilometres away from her school. Every day she walks to school and home again. How far does she walk everyday?	

Investigation   How far is it?

Feather 5 km
Crest 20 km
Beak 30 km
Wing 45 km

How far is it from Feather to Crest?

How far is it from Beak to Wing?

How far is it from Feather to Wing?

9 Area

Step 1

My strategies

1	Mia covered her book with blocks. Each row had 5 blocks and there were 3 rows. How many blocks did she use?	
2	Ava covered her book with blocks. She had 4 rows with 3 blocks in each row. How many blocks did she use?	
3	The chocolate bar is made of two columns of squares. Each column has 5 squares. How many squares are in the chocolate bar?	

Step 2

My strategies

1	Leigh used 4 cubes to cover her shape. How many cubes would she need if she doubled the area of her shape?	
2	Jacqui used used 6 cubes to cover her shape. How many cubes would she need if she cut her shape in half?	
3	How many cubes are needed to cover a shape of 4 cubes long and 3 cubes wide?	

Investigation — Halves and quarters

Draw hearts on 1/2 of the shape.   Colour 1/2 of the shape light blue.

Draw stars on 1/4 of the shape.   Colour 1/4 of the shape pink.

©Greg Purcell and Brilliant Publications
This page may be photocopied for use by the purchasing institution only.

10   Volume and capacity

Step 1

My strategies

1	Anna's model has 3 layers. Each layer has 4 cubes. How many cubes are in her model?	
2	Luke's model has 4 layers. Each layer has 10 blocks. How many blocks are in his model?	
3	I used 6 cupfuls of milk to fill the jug. How many cupfuls did I use altogether if I filled one jug and two extra cupfuls?	

Step 2

My strategies

1	Finn's model has 10 layers. Each layer has 5 cubes. How many cubes are in Finn's model?	
2	It took 6 cupfuls of water to fill a bottle. If 1/2 was poured out, how many cupfuls were left?	
3	4 cupfuls of juice half filled the big bottle. How many cupfuls would I need to fill the bottle?	

Investigation   Making cordial

One cupful of water has been poured into the jug.

1	Add 2 cupfuls of green cordial. Show the new level the jug will be filled to. Colour the new level green.
2	Add another cup of red cordial. Show the new level the jug will be filled to. Colour the new level red.
3	Add another 2 cupfuls of blue cordial. Show the new level the jug will be filled to. Colour the new level blue.

14   Maths Problems and Investigations 5–7 Year Olds   ©Greg Purcell and Brilliant Publications

11 Mass

Step 1

My strategies

1	Jo balanced a bottle of water with 2 apples. How many apples would she need to balance 2 bottles?	
2	Alan balanced a bottle of water with 4 blocks. How many blocks would he need to balance 3 bottles?	
3	Ayisha's birthday cake had a mass of 2 kilograms. What would its mass be if ½ was eaten?	

Step 2

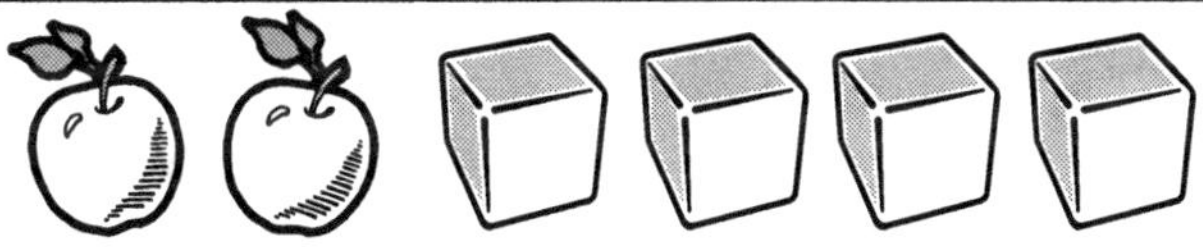

My strategies

1	2 apples balance 4 blocks. How many blocks would balance 4 apples?	
2	Each box has a mass of 2 kilograms. What would be the mass of 4 boxes?	
3	How much would 4 kilograms of tomatoes cost if they are £1.20 per kilogram?	

Investigation — What am I thinking of?

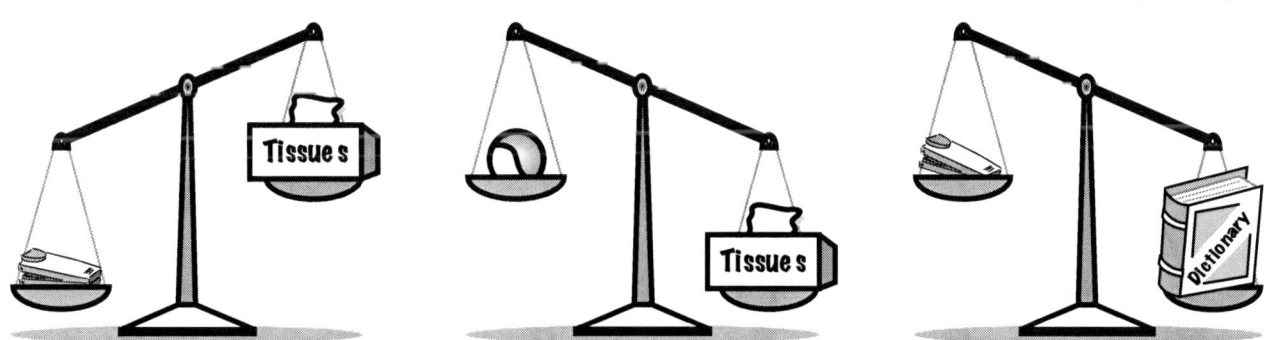

1	I am heavier than the **ball** but lighter than the **stapler**.	
2	I am lighter than the **book** but heavier than the **tissue box**.	
3	I am the lightest object on the balance scales.	

12 Time

Step 1

My strategies

1	Show what time Madison arrived at school. She left home at 8 o'clock and arrived at school one hour later.	
2	Show what time Jack ate his fruit. He arrived at school at 9 o'clock and ate his apple two hours later.	
3	Show what time Dylan arrived home. He left school at 3 o'clock, but didn't get home until 3 hours later.	

Step 2

My strategies

1	How long was Kaitlyn away? She left home at 4 o'clock and got home at 6 o'clock.	
2	When did Lucas arrive at the pool? He left home at **half past 8** and arrived at the pool **half an hour** later.	
3	When did Taylor get home? She left home at 7 o'clock and got home 4 hours later.	

Investigation   What time is it?

I am later than 1 o'clock.	I'm earlier than 10 o'clock.	I'm later than 9 o'clock.
I am earlier than 4 o'clock.	I'm later than 7 o'clock.	I'm before midday.
I am later than 2 o'clock.	I'm earlier than 9 o'clock.	I'm later than 10 o'clock.

13 Number

Step 1 35 ? 39   **My strategies**

1	The house numbers in the street go up by 2s. What is the number on the house between Number 35 and Number 39?	
2	Tim has six 10 pence coins. Use the pattern to help him count his money. 10p 20p 30p 40p 50p ☐p	
3	Simon is walking down the street. The house numbers go backwards by 2s. What house number is between 96 and 92?	

Step 2   0 5 10 15 20 25   **My strategies**

1	Max is skip counting by 5s and is up to 25. Kierra is skip counting by 10s and is up to 20. What is the next number they will both say?	
2	Noah made a number pattern. 35 30 ☐ 20 15 10 5 0 One number card fell off the board. What is the missing number in his pattern?	
3	Tim is 4 years older than Charlie. How old will Tim be when Charlie is 9?	

Investigation   Number puzzle

Place the numbers **3**, **6** and **8** in the circles so that the sum of each line is 15.

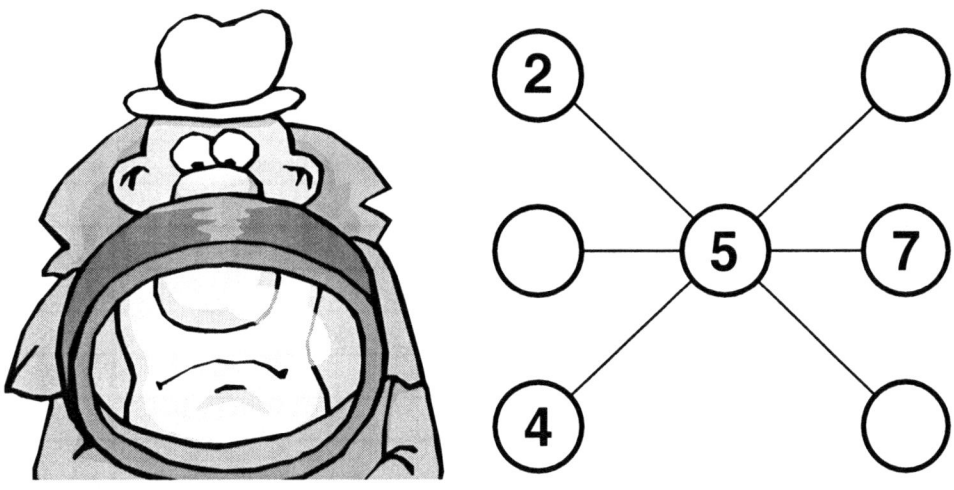

14 Addition

Step 1

My strategies

1	Lara collected 12 shells on Saturday and 7 on Sunday. How many shells did she collect altogether?	
2	Eve bought 15 pencils at one shop and 3 at another. How many pencils did she buy?	
3	Ananya scored 8 points in the first game and 6 the second game. How many points did she score altogether?	

Step 2

My strategies

1	Leo caught 13 fish and Finn caught 12 fish. How many fish did they catch altogether?	
2	Toby spent £25 at one shop and £14 at another shop. How much did he spend altogether?	
3	The canteen sold 34 hamburgers in the morning and 24 in the afternoon. How many hamburgers did they sell altogether?	

Investigation   Book club

Josh and Leah each have £20 to spend on their Book Club order.
Fill out the order forms showing 2 different orders that will cost £20.

Book club order form	
Name	*Josh*
Titles	Price
Total	

Book club order form	
Name	*Leah*
Titles	Price
Total	

15 Subtraction

Step 1

My strategies

1	Angus had 6 stickers but gave 2 away. How many stickers has he got left?	
2	There were 8 people at the party but 3 had to leave early. How many stayed until the party was over?	
3	Grace had 9 balloons but 5 blew away. How many has she got left?	

Step 2

My strategies

1	Mum made 10 cakes for the school picnic. How many are left if Ellen's friends ate 7 of them?	
2	20 toys were for sale at the shop. How many are left if 15 were sold?	
3	There were 18 sheep in the paddock. How many were black sheep if 13 were white?	

Investigation   Pizza

Tropical £11   Meat £12   Super £13   Vegetarian £14

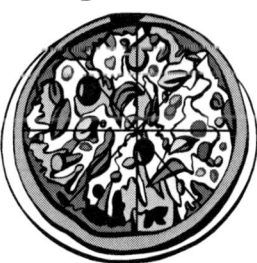   

How much change will each person get?

Eva tendered £10   £5   to pay for the £12 pizza. _____

Zac tendered £10   £10 to pay for the £11 pizza. _____

Max tendered £10   £5   to pay for the £13 pizza. _____

16 Multiplication

Step 1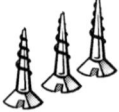

My strategies

1	Each tin contains 4 tennis balls. How many balls would there be in 3 tins?	
2	Each chair has 5 screws. How many screws are needed for 6 chairs?	
3	Tickets are £10 each. How much would 8 tickets cost?	

Step 2

My strategies

1	Each Christmas tree will have 9 stars. How many stars are needed to decorate 5 trees?	
2	Each hen laid 5 eggs. How many eggs would you get from 8 hens?	
3	A try is worth 5 points in rugby union. How many points did Caleb score if he kicked 7 goals?	

Investigation   How many cakes?

Each row on the tray has room for 5 cakes.

How many cakes would fit on 3 rows?	
How many cakes would fit on 4 rows?	
How many cakes would fit on 5 rows?	

17 Division

Step 1

My strategies

1	10 breadsticks were shared equally between 2 children. How many did each child get?	
2	Sienna and Lena shared a pack of 8 pencils equally. How many did each girl receive?	
3	Sam, Ava and Emily were given 9 marbles to share equally. How many will each person receive?	

Step 2

My strategies

1	Abbey arranged her 12 dolls into 3 equal groups. How many will be in each group?	
2	Mrs Johnson is dividing 20 children into 4 equal teams. How many will be in each team?	
3	Pop gave his 3 grandchildren £18 to share equally. How much will each person receive?	

Investigation — Share and share alike

Help share the 24 blocks.

24 blocks shared among 3 people. ☐

24 blocks shared among 4 people. ☐

24 blocks shared among 6 people. ☐

18 Fractions

Step 1

My strategies

1	Hannah is 12 years old. Molly is half her age. How old is Molly?	
2	1 out of every 4 children in our street plays soccer. There are 12 children in our street. How many play soccer?	
3	Hayley is 16 years old. Toby is a quarter of Hayley's age. How old is Toby?	

Step 2

My strategies

1	20 sausage rolls were sold at the canteen. Half had tomato sauce and half didn't. How many had sauce on them?	
2	Luke's bag has a mass of 16 kilograms. Adam's bag is only half as heavy. How heavy is Adam's bag?	
3	There are 20 people in our class. One-quarter ordered their lunch from the canteen. How many people ordered their lunch?	

Investigation   Sticker run

Our teacher Miss White has 20 **Well Done** stickers.
How many were given out?

½ were given out on Monday.

¼ were given out on Tuesday.

How many are left?

19 Data

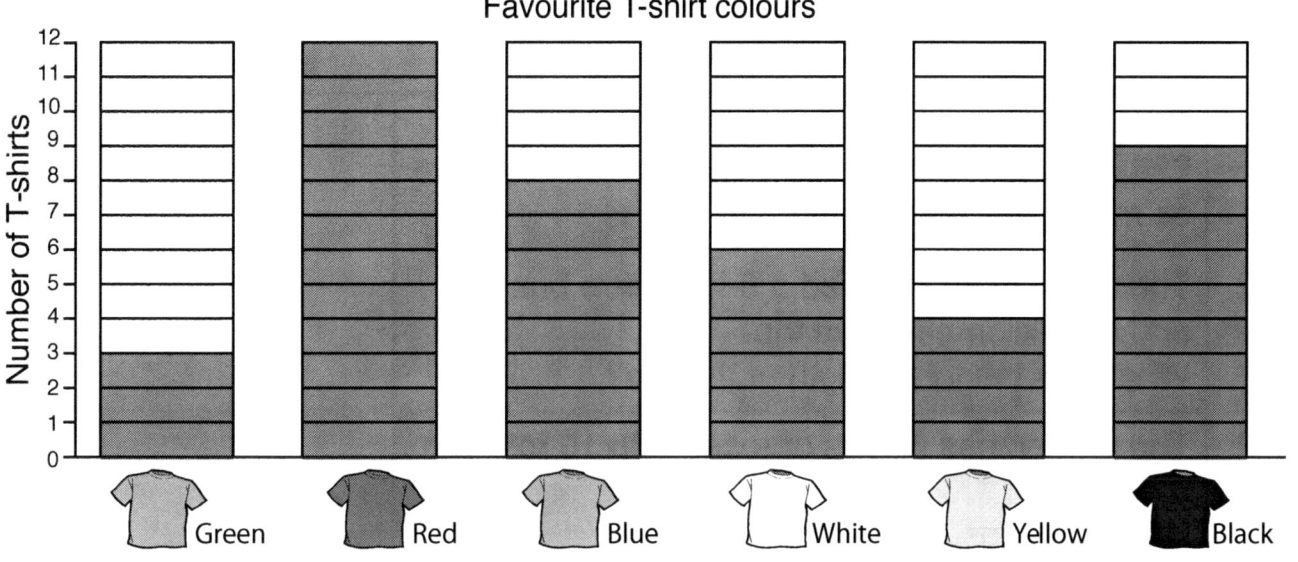

Step 1

My strategies

1	What is the most popular colour?	
2	What is the least popular colour?	
3	What is the difference between the most popular colour and the least popular colour?	

Step 2

My strategies

1	Which colour is twice as popular as white?	
2	Which colour is three times more popular than green?	
3	Which colour is half as popular as blue?	

Investigation — Our favourite colour

Ask your friends what their favourite colour is. Colour the T-shirt the most popular colour they chose.

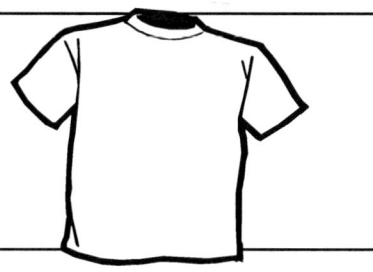

©Greg Purcell and Brilliant Publications   Maths Problems and Investigations 5–7 Year Olds   23
This page may be photocopied for use by the purchasing institution only.

20 Number operations

Step 1

My strategies

1	Grace has saved £35 and William has saved £26. How much more does William need to have as much as Grace?	
2	The trip to town included a 5-kilometre bus trip and a 29-kilometre train trip. What was the total length of the trip?	
3	The garden has 5 rows of roses with 10 roses in each row. How many roses are in the garden?	

Step 2

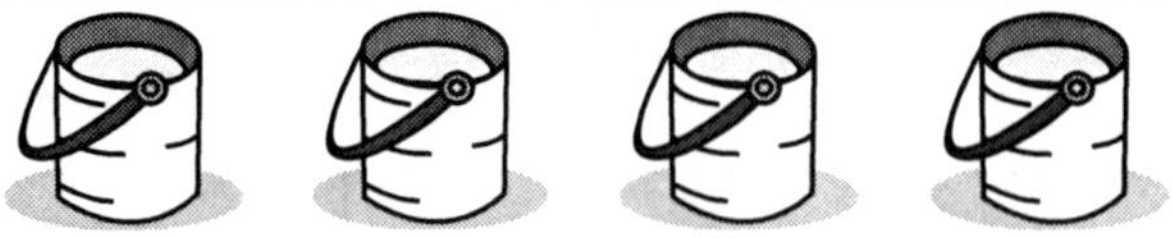

My strategies

1	20 litres of paint were poured into 4 tins. How many litres are in each tin?	
2	Jasper is going to buy 7 tickets to the movies. How much will he pay if the tickets are £4 each?	
3	All the children had to take their shoes off for their gymnastics class. Ricky counted 24 shoes. How many children were in the class?	

Investigation

Place the digits **1, 2, 3, 4** and **5** in the shapes so that the sum of the 3 numbers in both *horizontal* and *vertical* directions is the same.

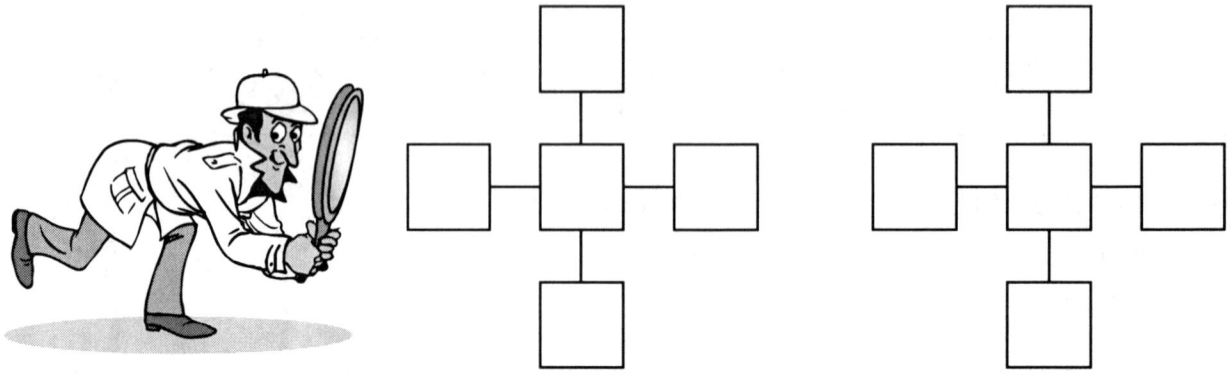

24 Maths Problems and Investigations 5–7 Year Olds

21 Patterns

Step 1 14, 16, 18, __ ?

My strategies

1	In the skip-counting pattern, Lena is ready to say her number. What number will she say if the 3 people before her said: 14, 16 and 18?	
2	In Darcy's skip-counting pattern, the last three numbers have been 35, 40 and 45. What is the next number?	
3	In the skip-counting pattern, Petra is ready to say her number. What number will she say if the 3 people before her said: 42, 40 and 38?	

Step 2

My strategies

1	When throwing the dice both girls got a total of 8 each. Lucy's throws a 2 and 6. What was Abbey's last throw if her first throw was 4?	
2	When throwing the dice both boys got a total of 9. Colin's throws were 6 and 3. What was Jack's last throw if his first throw was 5?	
3	When throwing the dice both girls got a total of 10. Melanie's throws were 5 and 5. What was Ava's last throw if her first throw was 6.	

Investigation   Matchstick puzzle

Take 4 sticks away to make 1 square.

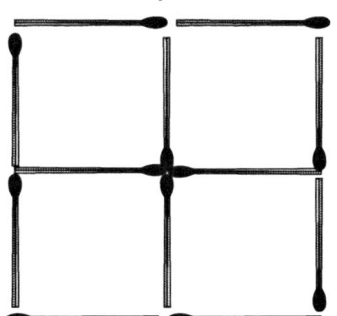

Take 2 sticks away to make 3 squares.

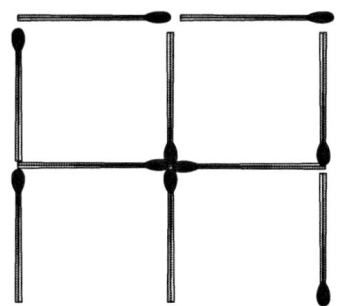

Take 2 sticks away to make 2 squares.

22 Length

Step 1

My strategies

1	The truck is 3 metres longer than Mum's car. Mum's car is 2 metres long. How long is the truck?	
2	The red post is 14 metres long. How long is the green post if it is 5 metres shorter?	
3	Two pieces of wood, each 4 metres long, were joined together. How long is the piece of wood now?	

Step 2

My strategies

1	Zoe jogged along the track for 12 kilometres and finished by walking another 5 kilometres. How long is the track?	
2	Each building brick is 20 centimetres tall. The fence is 4 bricks high. How tall is the fence?	
3	Jacqui lives 12 kilometres away from the netball courts. Lucy lives half that distance away. How far from the courts does Lucy live?	

Investigation — Whose house is it?

Holly's house is 5 cm away from the school. Colour her house pink.

Anna's house is 4 cm away from the school. Colour her house blue.

Ruby's house is 3 cm away from the school. Colour her house red.

Hint: Measure from the black dots.

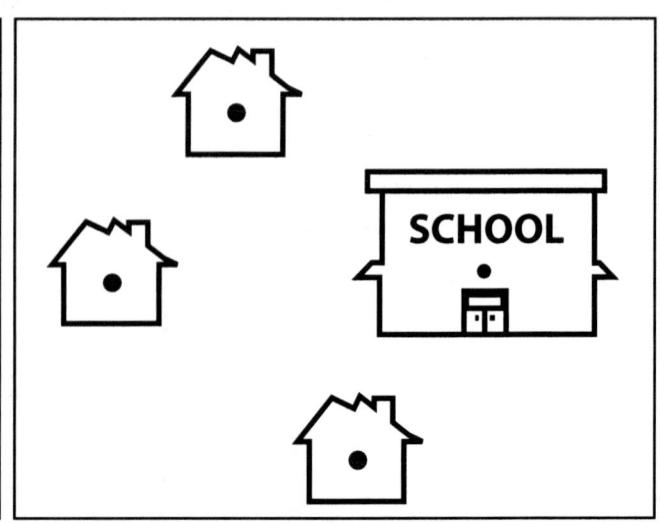

23 Area

Step 1  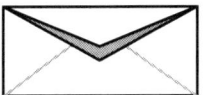  ? **My strategies**

1	Lily covered the table with place mats. She made 5 rows with 6 mats in each row. How many mats did she use?	
2	Grace's board game is made up of squares. There are 10 rows with 10 squares in each row. How many squares are on the board?	
3	Max needed 12 envelopes to cover his desk. His teacher's desk is twice the area. How many envelopes are needed to cover her desk?	

Step 2  ? **My strategies**

1	How many place mats are are needed to cover a shape 6 place mats long and 5 place mats wide?	
2	7 gym mats were used to cover a quarter of a basketball court. How many mats would be needed to cover all the court?	
3	Triangular pattern blocks are half the size of rectangular blocks. If I used 9 rectangular blocks to cover a shape, how many triangular blocks will I need?	

Investigation — Seeing stars

Draw 3 straight lines in each box so that each star is in a separate area.

24 Volume and capacity

Step 1

My strategies

1	12 litres have been poured into a tank but it is still only half full. How many litres are needed to fill the tank?	
2	Callum's cube is 3 layers high. Each layer is made with 3 building blocks. How many blocks are in the cube?	
3	The fish tank can hold 60 litres. How much more water will fit in if 45 litres have already been poured in?	

Step 2

My strategies

1	4 people each drank 2 litres of water during the day. How much did they drink altogether?	
2	3 rooms were painted using 5 litres of paint. How many litres would be needed to paint 15 rooms?	
3	The pool man told us to pour 1½ buckets of cleaner into the pool. How many litres is this if a bucket holds 10-litres?	

Investigation — Hole in my roof

Lisa's roof leaks.
The hole is getting bigger every day.
She uses 10-litre buckets to collect the water.
Calculate how much she collected each day.

Friday ▯ = ☐ litres

Saturday ▯▯ = ☐ litres

Sunday ▯▯▯ = ☐ litres

25 Mass

Step 1

My strategies

1	The builder noticed that 1 bolt balanced 4 screws. How many bolts would balance 8 screws?	
2	A carpenter noticed that 1 bolt balanced 5 nails. How many bolts would balance 10 nails?	
3	1 clump of Plasticine balanced 3 carrots. How many clumps of Plasticine are needed to balance 6 carrots?	

Step 2

My strategies

1	1 pumpkin has a mass of 2 kilograms. What would be the mass of 2 similar pumpkins?	
2	How heavy is the load if it contains a 2 kilogram pumpkin and 3 kilograms of carrots?	
3	4 screws balance 5 nails. How many nails are needed to balance 8 screws?	

Investigation   Of equal balance!

Use the scales to help make the sentences true.

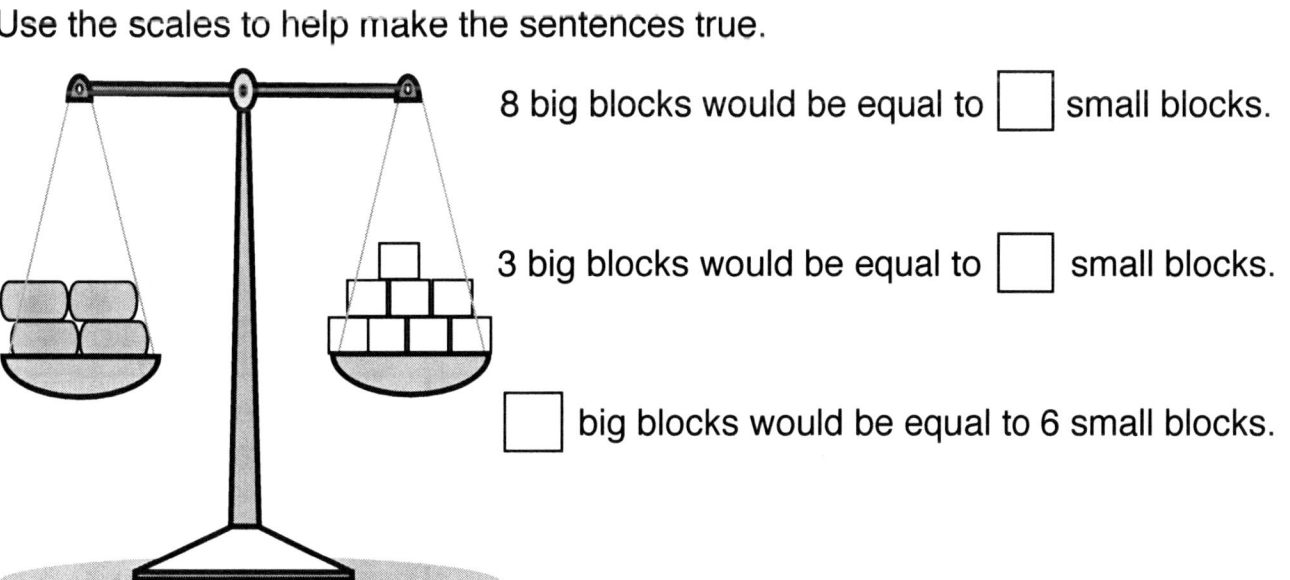

8 big blocks would be equal to ☐ small blocks.

3 big blocks would be equal to ☐ small blocks.

☐ big blocks would be equal to 6 small blocks.

26 Time

Step 1

My strategies

1	Show what time Oscar got home. He left school at 4:30 and got home half an hour later.	
2	Show what time the game finished. It started at 8:30 and finished 1 hour later.	
3	When did Jenna get home from school? She left school at 3:30 and got home half an hour later.	

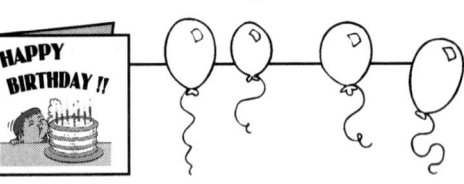

Step 2

My strategies

1	When did Riley's birthday party finish? It began at 2 o'clock and finished 2½ hours later.	
2	What time did Ebony arrive home? She left her cousin's house at 5 o'clock and got home 4 hours later.	
3	When did Anna get home? She left home at 9:30 and returned home 2 hours later.	

Investigation — What time is it?

 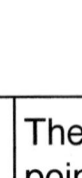  

The minute hand is halfway around the clock. The hour hand is halfway between 3 and 4.	The minute hand is pointing at 12. The hour hand is halfway between 12 and 6.	The minute hand is halfway around the clock. The hour hand is halfway between 10 and 11.

Maths Problems and Investigations 5–7 Year Olds

27 Number

Step 1

My strategies

1	Create the largest number possible using these three number cards: ④ ⑤ ⑥	
2	Which number is one less than four hundred and twenty-six?	
3	Create the smallest number possible using these three number cards: ⑨ ⑤ ②	

Step 2

My strategies

1	Eric needs about £18 for his trip to the city. Round this off to show how many £10 notes he should take.	
2	Jack is counting by 4s. Jill is counting by 5s. They both stared at zero. What is the first number they will both count?	
3	Dad arranges his shirts in a colour pattern. Every 4th shirt is blue. If he has 9 shirts, how many blue ones will there be?	

Investigation — Staircase numbers

Natalia has created some staircase numbers.
Draw the 3rd and 5th staircase numbers in the pattern.

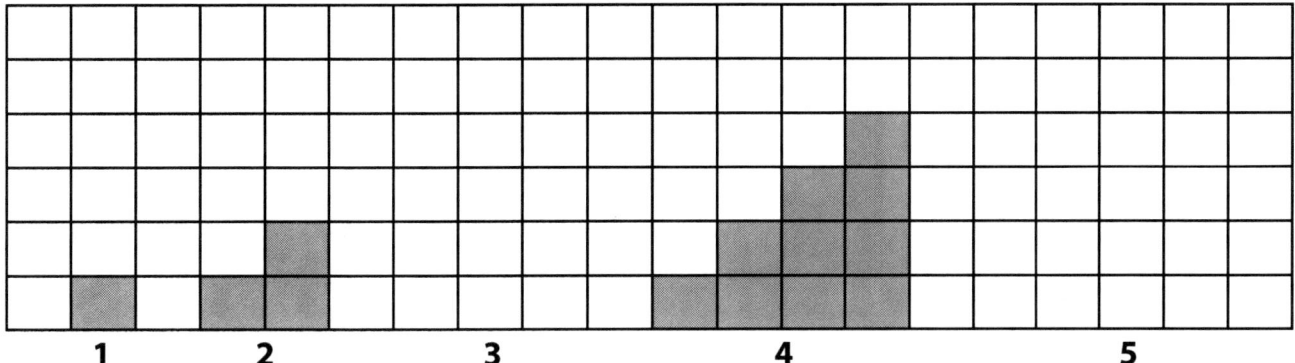

©Greg Purcell and Brilliant Publications   Maths Problems and Investigations 5–7 Year Olds
This page may be photocopied for use by the purchasing institution only.

28 Addition

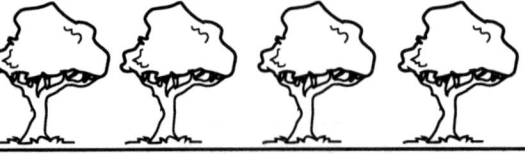

Step 1

		My strategies
1	How much money does Amy have? She has £42 in the bank and £36 at home.	
2	53 trees were planted this year and 46 were planted last year. How many were planted over the last two years?	
3	How many days was Dad away on his trip? He was away for 23 days in March and 24 days in April.	

Step 2

		My strategies
1	How many cards does Lucas have? He had 49 cards and bought another 26.	
2	How many drinks were sold at the kiosk? 47 were sold on Saturday and 38 on Sunday.	
3	What was Kayla's total score in the cricket matches. She scored 65 in the first game and 47 in the second match.	

Investigation — Magic square

In a magic square every row of numbers, every column of numbers and every diagonal line of numbers add to give the same total.

Use the numbers on the juggler's balls to complete the magic square.

The total of each line on this magic square is **15**.

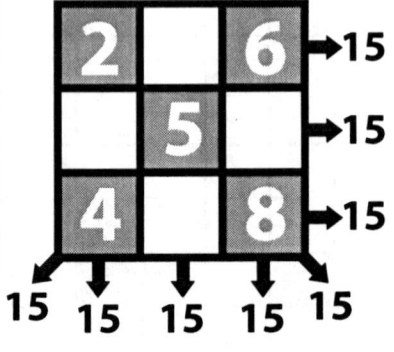

32   Maths Problems and Investigations 5–7 Year Olds   ©Greg Purcell and Brilliant Publications
This page may be photocopied for use by the purchasing institution only.

29 Subtraction

Step 1

My strategies

1	One box has 45 chocolates and the other has 23 chocolates. What is the difference between the two boxes?	
2	Mason had 65 marbles but lost 34 in a game. How many does he have left?	
3	Lily has 46 different plants in her garden. Rose has 23 in her garden. How many more plants does Lily have?	

Step 2

My strategies

1	Each team in the netball competition has to play 15 games. The Swifts have won 5 and lost 3. How many games are left?	
2	Jahmel scored 43 points in the final and Will scored 35 points. How many more points did Jahmel score?	
3	Kate used 54 shape tiles in her pattern. Grace used 19 fewer tiles than Kate. How many tiles did Grace use?	

Investigation Mobile number

Three people want to buy a mobile phone. How much more does each person need.

Tom has £63	Eve has £52	Max has £79

30   Multiplication

Step 1

My strategies

1	Carly has 3 sets of swap cards. Each set contains 5 cards. How many cards does she own?	
2	4 people each donated £5 to the school. How much money was donated?	
3	10 people entered the singing contest. Each person had to sing 3 songs. How many songs did the judges listen to?	

Step 2

My strategies

1	How much did the shopkeeper collect? He sold nine toys, each worth £5.	
2	How many spaces did Stella move on the board game if she threw 3 sixes in a row?	
3	David goes to swimming training four times a week. How far does he swim each week if he swims 4 kilometres each session?	

Investigation   Double-decker ice creams

Ice creams come in 3 flavours at Dylan's shop.

When Dylan makes double-decker ice-creams he mixes the flavours.

Colour the ice creams to show the different combinations he can make using 2 flavours.

Strawberry   Vanilla   Chocolate

Maths Problems and Investigations 5–7 Year Olds   ©Greg Purcell and Brilliant Publications
This page may be photocopied for use by the purchasing institution only.

31 Division

Step 1

My strategies

1	How many cakes did each person receive if 12 cakes were shared equally among 3 children?	
2	15 people arrived for dinner. How many would sit at each table if there were 5 tables and the same number sat at each table?	
3	£20 was to be shared equally among 4 people. How much will each person receive?	

Step 2

My strategies

1	A 12 metre rope was cut into four equal pieces. How long is each piece?	
2	A group of 15 people ordered 3 taxi cabs. How many people sat in each taxi if the people were evenly distributed?	
3	Flynn drew 18 pictures for his 6-page picture book. How many pictures did he put on each page if there were an equal number of pictures on each of the pages?	

Investigation — Basketball points

The Stingers scored 40 points in the final.
Show different ways the points were scored.

4 people scored an equal number of points.

5 people scored an equal number of points.

2 people scored an equal number of points.

32 Fractions

Step 1 **My strategies**

1	Hannah bought 12 eggs but dropped ¼ of them. How many did she drop?	
2	In the netball game our team scored 20 points. Ashley scored half of the team's points. How many points did Ashley score?	
3	The coach put out 20 balls to play with but ¼ of them were flat. How many were flat?	

Step 2 **My strategies**

1	The rope on the boat is 16 metres long. One of the sailors cut off one quarter of it. How much was cut off?	
2	Mum baked 20 cakes for the school fete. Dad bought one quarter of them. How many did Dad buy?	
3	24 children do gymnastics. One quarter of them are boys. How many boys do gymnastics?	

Investigation   Unusual split

Jett has divided one square into two equal parts. Divide the other squares into unusual halves.

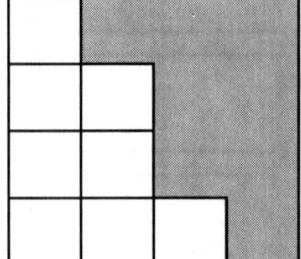 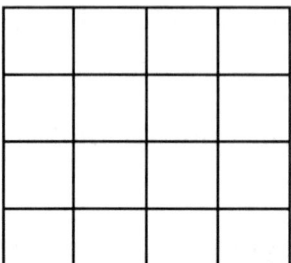 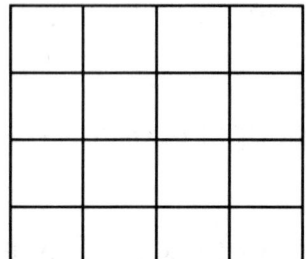 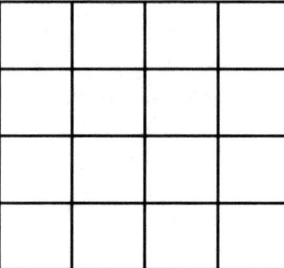

33 Data

Ice cream flavours

(Bar chart: Banana 10, Lemon 15, Mango 40, Pineapple 20, Strawberry 45)

Step 1

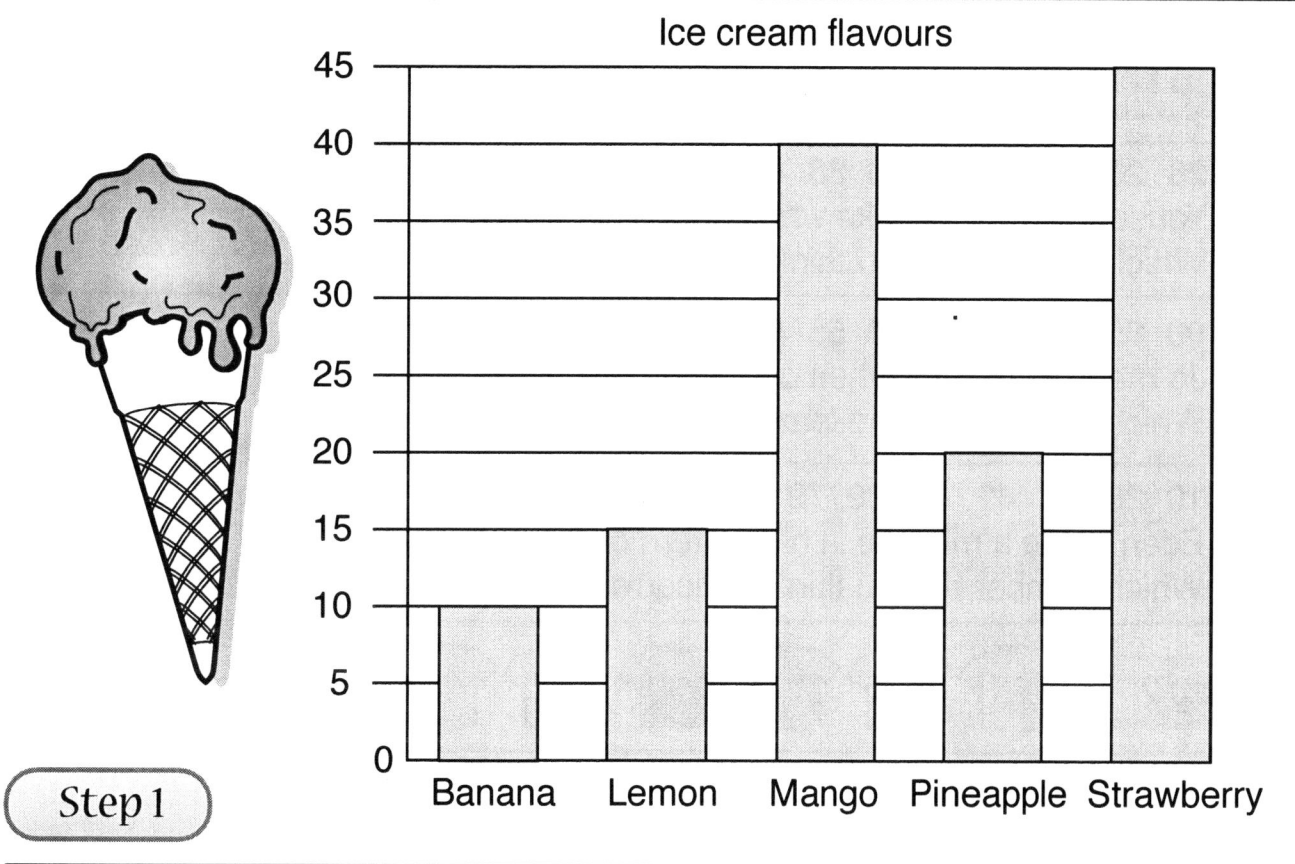

1	What is the most popular flavour?	
2	What is the least popular flavour?	
3	What is the difference between the most popular flavour and the least popular flavour?	

Step 2

My strategies

1	Which flavour is twice as popular as banana?	
2	Which flavour is three times more popular than lemon?	
3	Which flavour is half as popular as mango?	

Investigation — Our favourite flavour

Ask your friends what their favourite flavour ice cream is. Colour the columns on a graph to match your data.

34 Patterns

Step 1

My strategies

1	26 28 30 32 35 36 38 40 42 Yousef made a mistake when counting by 2s. Which number do you think is incorrect?	
2	90 85 80 75 70 60 55 50 45 Jo made a mistake when counting backwards. Which number did she leave out?	
3	19 28 39 49 59 69 79 89 99 Eden made a mistake in his pattern of tens. Which number do you think is incorrect?	

Step 2

My strategies

1	Nine girls are in the netball team. Every 3rd girl has a pony-tail. Would the 5th girl have a pony-tail?	
2	12 pieces of fruit were put on the shelf. Every 5th piece was green. Would the 10th piece be green?	
3	Dad has 10 work shirts. Every 4th shirt is red. Would the 8th shirt be red or another colour?	

Investigation   Stepping stones

There are 36 stepping stones in the garden.
- Leo stepped on every second stone.
- Dad stepped on every third stone.

Colour the stones that both Leo and Dad landed on.

Start

Finish

35 Addition

Step 1

My strategies

1	The bus took 30 children to the circus and then came back to collect another 30 children. How many children went to the circus?	
2	40 boxes of dog food were in the shop and another 40 were kept in the storeroom. How many boxes were there altogether?	
3	Emma got 50 words correct in the first spelling quiz and 50 in the second quiz. What was her total score?	

Step 2

My strategies

1	56 metres of rope were joined with another 23 metres to make one long rope. How long is the rope now?	
2	How much did Lucy spend if she spent £36 at the fruit shop and £26 at the butcher shop?	
3	The truck driver has two parcels to deliver. One had a mass of 35 kilograms and the other 27 kilograms. What was the total mass of his load?	

Investigation   How to make 100

Find four pairs of numbers that have a total of 100.

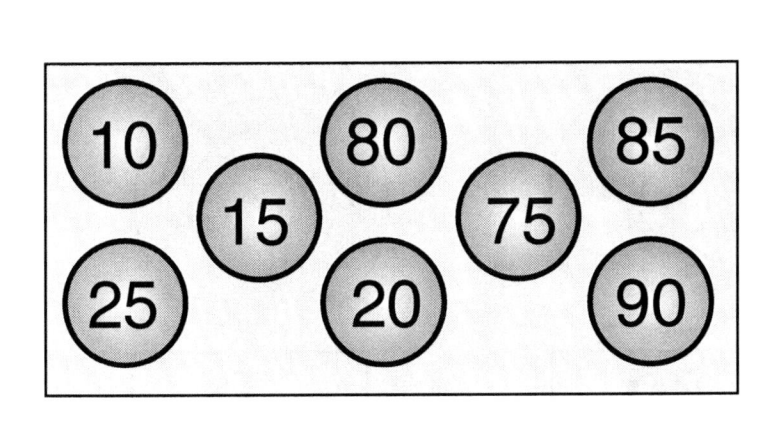

10   80   85
  15   75
25   20   90

☐ + ☐ = 100

☐ + ☐ = 100

☐ + ☐ = 100

☐ + ☐ = 100

36 Subtraction

Step 1

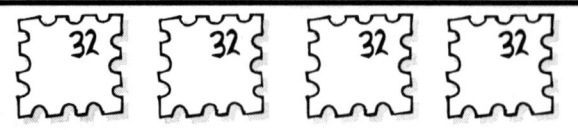

My strategies

1	Max has a collection of 25 stamps. 14 are British and the rest are from overseas. How many overseas stamps does he own?	
2	54 children attended the camp. How many were girls if there were 23 boys?	
3	Lucy had £40 but spent £12. How much has she got left?	

Step 2

My strategies

1	Our teacher had 90 stickers but has already used 60 of them. How many does she have left?	
2	Connor wants to buy an games console for £88. How much more does he need if he only has £23?	
3	The market stall had 43 T-shirts and sold 25 of them. How many were not sold?	

Investigation — Bull's eye

Below each target is each person's total score. Draw in the missing arrows on each board so that the total scores match those below.

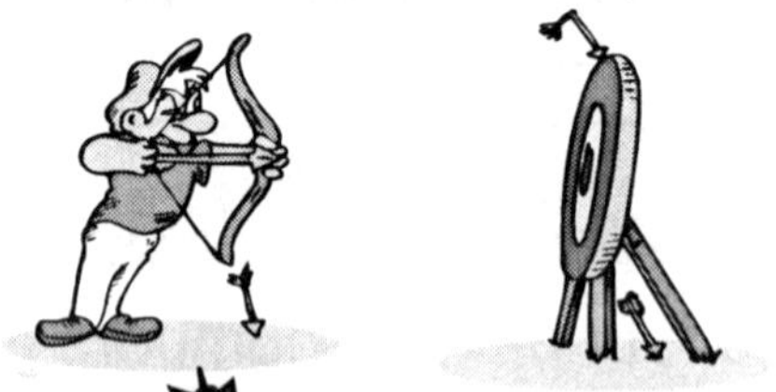

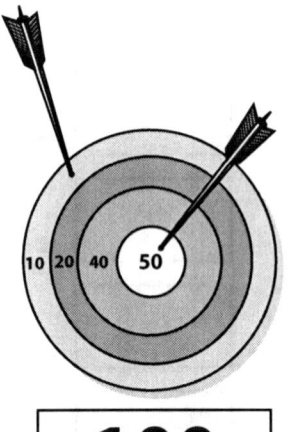

100 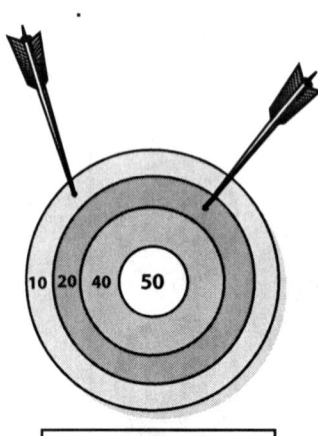 **80** 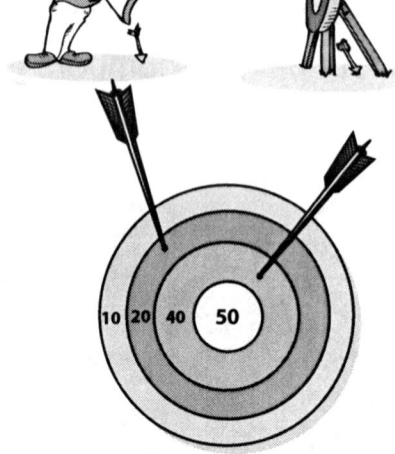 **70**

Maths Problems and Investigations 5–7 Year Olds ©Greg Purcell and Brilliant Publications
This page may be photocopied for use by the purchasing institution only.

37   Multiplication

Step 1

My strategies

1	Each packet contains 5 biscuits. Charlie bought 2 packets. How many biscuits did Charlie buy?	
2	Mohamed bought 4 train tickets. Each ticket costs £2. How much did he spend?	
3	Each taxi had 5 passengers. How many passengers were there if there were 3 taxis?	

Step 2

My strategies

1	We have 5 sports teams at school. There are 10 people in each team. How many people are in sports teams?	
2	Jake swims 5 kilometres 5 times a week. How far does he swim each week?	
3	Mum paid £9 each for 5 tickets to the movie. How much did she spend?	

Investigation   Dad's new clothes

£6   £12   £4

Draw and decorate the number of socks he could buy with £36.	Draw and decorate the number of shirts he could buy with £36.	Draw and decorate the number of ties he could buy with £36.

38 Division

Step 1

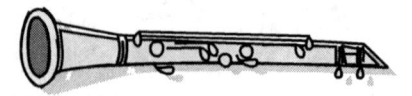

My strategies

1	12 sets of musical instruments were shared between 2 classes. How many sets of instruments did each class receive?	
2	20 Easter eggs were divided equally into 4 groups. How many were in each group?	
3	It cost Jessica £30 to pay for 10 tickets. How much was each ticket?	

Step 2

My strategies

1	15 tins of cat food were evenly placed on 5 shelves. How many were placed on each shelf?	
2	If 24 comic books were shared evenly among 4 people, how many would each person get?	
3	It took Madison 5 weeks to save £25. Each week she saved the same amount. How much did she save each week?	

Investigation   Saving up

Dylan has saved £12.

Calculate how much each person has saved.

Clues

Dylan has saved four times as much as Paul.
How much has Paul saved?

Flynn has saved twice as much as Paul.
How much has Flynn saved?

Dylan has saved three times as much as Tyler.
How much has Tyler saved?

39 Fractions

Step 1

My strategies

1	One quarter of the 12 pencils were broken. How many broken pencils were there?	
2	20 children ordered ice creams. Half ordered chocolate flavour. How many ordered chocolate?	
3	The toy Tom wants to buy costs £8. His mum said she would give him one quarter of the money. How much is his mum going to give him?	

Step 2

My strategies

1	24 people voted for their favourite colour. One out of every four voted for red. How many chose red as their favourite colour?	
2	A new games console is £100. Grace has half this much. How much money does Grace have?	
3	One quarter of the shape tiles are squares. If there are 40 shape tiles, how many are squares?	

Investigation — One good turn

Volkswagen cars have this symbol on their wheels.

What would the symbol look like every ¼ turn?

Complete the turning pattern to show what the symbol would look like as it turns.

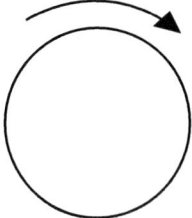

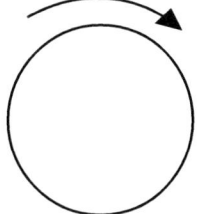

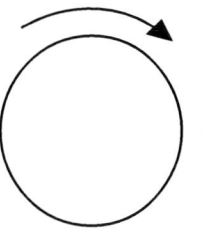

40 Data

Animals on the farm

Cows: 🐄🐄🐄🐄🐄 (5)
Sheep: 🐑🐑🐑🐑🐑🐑🐑🐑 (8)
Goats: 🐐🐐🐐🐐🐐 (5)
Horses: 🐴🐴🐴🐴🐴 (5)
Pigs: 🐖🐖🐖🐖🐖🐖🐖 (7)

Step 1

1	How many animals are on the farm?	
2	Which two groups have a combined total of 15?	
3	Which three groups have a combined total of 15?	

Step 2

My strategies

1	How many sheep would the farmer have if he doubled the number of sheep?	
2	How many goats would the farmer have if he tripled the number of goats?	
3	How many animals would be left if half the animals were sold?	

Investigation — Piggy bank

Calculate the value of these animals on the farm.

- cows are worth £50 each   £ ☐
- horses are worth £100 each   £ ☐
- pigs are worth £20 each   £ ☐

Answers Units 1–10

Unit 1

Step 1
1. 30
2. 5
3. 18

Step 2
1. 20
2. 38
3. 50

Investigation
14, 25

Unit 2

Step 1
1. 9
2. £5
3. 10

Step 2
1. 13
2. 13
3. 16

Investigation
12 and 8, 6 and 14, 17 and 3

Unit 3

Step 1
1. £5
2. 2
3. 4

Step 2
1. 7
2. 6
3. 10

Investigation
11, 11, 10

Unit 4

Step 1
1. 8
2. 12
3. 10

Step 2
1. 6
2. 12
3. 15

Investigation
15, 20, 25

Unit 5

Step 1
1. 4
2. 5
3. 3

Step 2
1. 3
2. £4
3. 4

Investigation
4 each
3 each
2 each

Unit 6

Step 1
1. 4
2. 3
3. 2

Step 2
1. 5
2. 9
3. 8

Investigation
8
4
yes

Unit 7

Step 1
1. 3
2. 7
3. 1

Step 2
1. 4
2. 2
3. 30

Unit 8

Step 1
1. 9 m
2. 6 cm
3. 9 m

Step 2
1. 10 cm
2. 2 m
3. 6 km

Investigation
15 km, 15 km, 40 km

Unit 9

Step 1
1. 15
2. 12
3. 10

Step 2
1. 8
2. 3
3. 12

Investigation
Two quarters should have hearts.
One quarter should have stars.
Two quarters should be shaded light blue.
One quarter of the shape should be shaded pink.

Unit 10

Step 1
1. 12
2. 40
3. 8

Step 2
1. 50
2. 3
3. 8

Investigation

©Greg Purcell and Brilliant Publications
This page may be photocopied for use by the purchasing institution only.

Answers Units 11–21

Unit 11

Step 1
1. 4
2. 12
3. 1 kg

Step 2
1. 8
2. 8 kg
3. £4.80

Investigation
Tissues, Stapler, Ball

Unit 12

Step 1
1. 9 o'clock
2. 11 o'clock
3. 6 o'clock

Step 2
1. 2 hours
2. 9 o'clock
3. 11 o'clock

Investigation
3 o'clock, 8 o'clock, 11 o'clock

Unit 13

Step 1
1. 37
2. 60p
3. 94

Step 2
1. 30
2. 25
3. 13

Investigation

Unit 14

Step 1
1. 19
2. 18
3. 14

Step 2
1. 25
2. £39
3. 58

Investigation
Josh – 'My Best Friend', 'The Missing Millions' and 'I Thought I Saw a Dinosaur'.
Leah – 'Slime and Grime', 'World Atlas' and 'I Thought I Saw a Dinosaur'.

Unit 15

Step 1
1. 4
2. 5
3. 4

Step 2
1. 3
2. 5
3. 5

Investigation
Eva £3, Zac £9, Max £2

Unit 16

Step 1
1. 12
2. 30
3. £80

Step 2
1. 45
2. 40
3. 35

Investigation
15, 20, 25

Unit 17

Step 1
1. 5
2. 4
3. 3

Step 2
1. 4
2. 5
3. £6

Investigation
8, 6, 4

Unit 18

Step 1
1. 6
2. 3
3. 4

Step 2
1. 10
2. 8 kg
3. 5

Investigation
10, 5, 5

Unit 19

Step 1
1. Red
2. Green
3. 9

Step 2
1. Red
2. Black
3. Yellow

Investigation
Own choice

Unit 20

Step 1
1. £9
2. 34 km
3. 50

Step 2
1. 5 l
2. £28
3. 12

Investigation

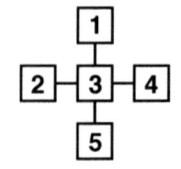

Unit 21

Step 1
1. 20
2. 50
3. 36

Maths Problems and Investigations 5–7 Year Olds   ©Greg Purcell and Brilliant Publications
This page may be photocopied for use by the purchasing institution only.

Answers — Units 21-30

Step 2
1. 4
2. 4
3. 4

Investigation

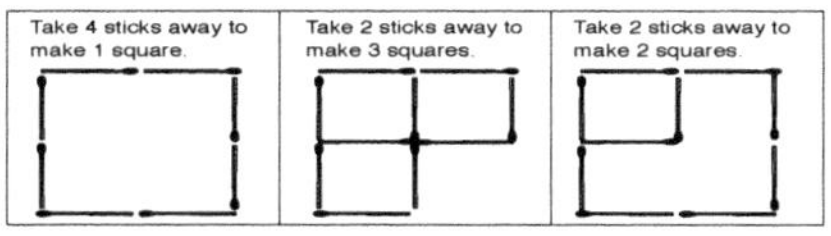

Take 4 sticks away to make 1 square.
Take 2 sticks away to make 3 squares.
Take 2 sticks away to make 2 squares.

Unit 22

Step 1
1. 5 m
2. 9 m
3. 8 m

Step 2
1. 17 km
2. 80 cm
3. 6 km

Investigation

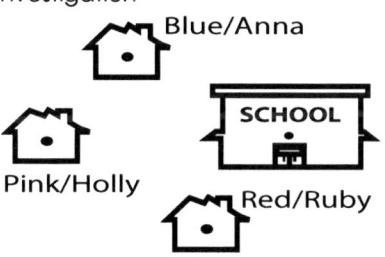

Blue/Anna
Pink/Holly
SCHOOL
Red/Ruby

Unit 23

Step 1
1. 30
2. 100
3. 24

Step 2
1. 30
2. 28
3. 18

Investigation

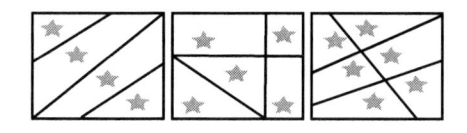

Unit 24

Step 1
1. 24 l
2. 9
3. 15 l

Step 2
1. 8 l
2. 25 l
3. 15 l

Investigation
Friday – 10 l, Saturday – 20 l, Sunday – 30 l

Unit 25

Step 1
1. 2
2. 2
3. 2

Step 2
1. 4 kg
2. 5 kg
3. 10

Investigation
16, 6, 3

Unit 26

Step 1
1. 5 o'clock
2. 9:30
3. 4 o'clock

Step 2
1. 4:30
2. 9 o'colock
3. 11:30

Investigation
3:30, 9 o'clock, 10:30

Unit 27

Step 1
1. 654
2. 425
3. 259

Step 2
1. £20, Two £10 notes
2. 20
3. 2

Investigation

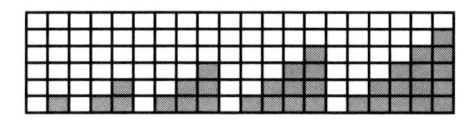

Unit 28

Step 1
1. £78
2. 99
3. 47

Step 2
1. 75
2. 85
3. 112

Investigation

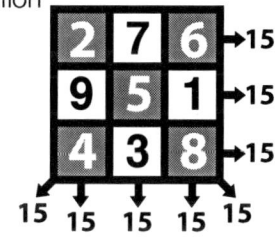

2	7	6	→15
9	5	1	→15
4	3	8	→15

15 15 15 15 15

Unit 29

Step 1
1. 22
2. 31
3. 23

Step 2
1. 7
2. 8
3. 35

Investigation
Tom £32, Eve £43, Max £16

Unit 30

Step 1
1. 15
2. £20
3. 30

Step 2
1. £45
2. 18
3. 16 km

Investigation
SV, SC, VS, VC, CV, CS

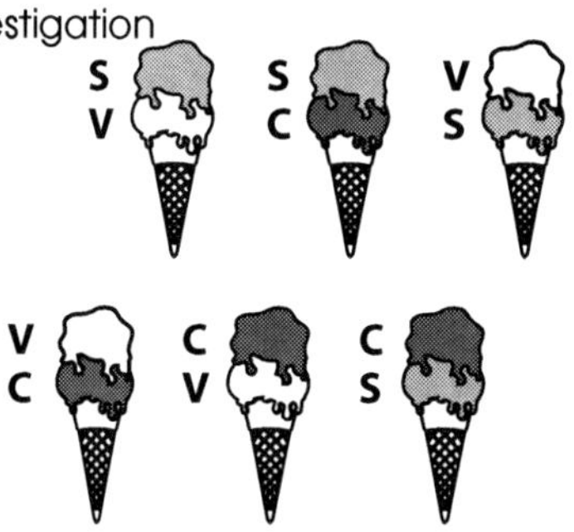

©Greg Purcell and Brilliant Publications
This page may be photocopied for use by the purchasing institution only.

Maths Problems and Investigations 5-7 Year Olds 47

Answers — Units 31–40

Unit 31

Step 1
1. 4
2. 3
3. £5

Step 2
1. 3 m
2. 5
3. 3

Investigation
10, 8, 20

Unit 32

Step 1
1. 3
2. 10
3. 5

Step 2
1. 4 m
2. 5
3. 6

Investigation

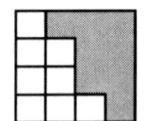

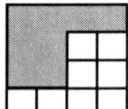

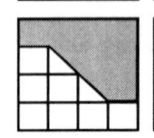

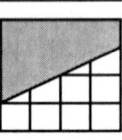

Unit 33

Step 1
1. Strawberry
2. Banana
3. 35

Step 2
1. Pineapple
2. Strawberry
3. Pineapple

Investigation
Own choice

Unit 34

Step 1
1. 35
2. 65
3. 28

Step 2
1. No
2. Yes
3. Red

Investigation

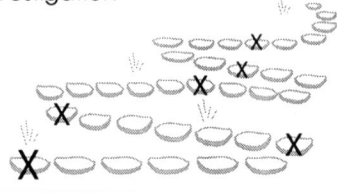

Unit 35

Step 1
1. 60
2. 80
3. 100

Step 2
1. 79 m
2. £62
3. 62 kg

Investigation
80 + 20, 75 + 25, 90 + 10, 85 + 15

Unit 36

Step 1
1. 11
2. 31
3. £28

Step 2
1. 30
2. £65
3. 18

Investigation

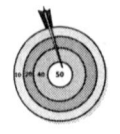

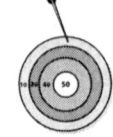

Unit 37

Step 1
1. 10
2. £8
3. 15

Step 2
1. 50
2. 25 km
3. £45

Investigation
6 pairs of socks, 3 shirts, 9 ties

Unit 38

Step 1   Step 2
1. 6   1. 3
2. 5   2. 6
3. £3   3. £5

Investigation
Dylan £12, Paul £3, Flynn £6, Tyler £4

Unit 39

Step 1   Step 2
1. 3   1. 6
2. 10   2. £50
3. £2   3. 10

Investigation

Unit 40

Step 1
1. 30
2. Sheep and pigs
3. Cows, goats and horses

Step 2
1. 16
2. 15
3. 15

Investigation
Cows £250, Horses £500, Pigs £140

48   Maths Problems and Investigations 5–7 Year Olds   ©Greg Purcell and Brilliant Publications
This page may be photocopied for use by the purchasing institution only.